Galapagos: *Islas Encantadas*

Pinta

Genovesa

Marchena

Wolf Volcano

1707

Darwin Volcano

San Salvador

Cerro Cowan

La Cumbre Volcano

Alcedo Volcano

Urbina Bay

Fernandina

Santa Cruz

Cerro Crocker

San Cristobal

Sierra Negra Volcano

Pto. Ayora

Santa Fe

Cerro Azul

Pto. Villamil

Puerto Baquerizo Moreno

Isabela

Santa Maria

Española

Galapagos: *Islas Encantadas*

poems by Michelle M. Tokarczyk

SHANTI ARTS PUBLISHING
BRUNSWICK, MAINE

Galapagos: *Islas Encantadas*

Published by Shanti Arts Publishing
Designed by Shanti Arts Designs

All photographs by Paul J. Groncki and used with his permission except for
the following: (title page) Daniel Feher, Map of Galapagos Islands (Ecuador,
South America), freeworldmaps.net. Wikimedia Commons. CC BY-SA 2.5;
(38) istock.com/SL_Photography; (41) istock.com/duncan1890; (43)
istock.com/Franz Schallmeiner (44) istock.com/Goddard_Photography.

Shanti Arts LLC
193 Hillside Road
Brunswick, Maine 04011
shantiarts.com

Printed in the United States of America

ISBN: 978-1-956056-70-9 (softcover)

Library of Congress Control Number: 2022951767

To the memory of my mother,
Florence Roberts Tokarczyk

Contents

Acknowledgments

Thanks to poetry workshop members Paola Corso, Cheryl J. Fish, Florence Homolka, and Elinor Mattern for their careful reading and constructive feedback. I'm indebted to Laura Orem for feedback on drafts of both "The Voyage Out" poems. For sharing her love and experience of birding, thanks to Christine Youngberg. Thanks to Marjorie Shaffer for identifying birds in my many pictures. Tim Hurson and Franca Leeson recommended Lindblad Expeditions' voyage to the Galapagos. I am grateful to Lindblad for an extraordinary voyage and to the government of Ecuador for its stewardship of the Galapagos. William Blake's *Songs of Innocence and Experience* inspired me to write about subjects from two vantage points—wonder and realism. Jeanie Murphy of Goucher College encouraged my study of Spanish. Juan Vallejo of Idlewild Language classes helped me to further develop my skills. Paul J. Groncki's photography captures the natural beauty of the Galapagos and the uniqueness of its animals. And, as always, I thank him, my husband, for his continued love and encouragement. For technical advice and assistance, I thank Jen Vernon, Donald Partyka, and Mitch Firestone.

I also wish to acknowledge the previous publication of some poems:
Earth's Daughters: "The Post Office Barrel: Experience"
Qutub Minar Review: "Reconsidering Coleridge's Albatross"
Unearthed: "The Post Office Barrel: Innocence"
The Raven's Perch: "The Voyage Out: The Backstory" and "The Voyage Out: To the Galapagos"

The Voyage Out: To the Galapagos

Fueled with visions of giant tortoises
and blue-footed boobies, I lace up my boots.
A surprise snowstorm lurks just hours away;
we rush out to the cab so we can fly
to the Islas Encantadas.

I need to walk other shores, to meet species
that have never seen enough of humans to fear.
If only our cabbie can drive well enough to steer
through Friday's afternoon streets.

At the airport night cocoons the terminal.
A child yells "*nieve!*" I trust the work of de-icing
as we board the plane. Unfrozen, we fly to Miami
where warmth permeates our doubts. Two more flights:
the sights of Guayaquil, a customs line coiling
through a room. Spanish-challenged, sleep-deprived,
we arrive on San Cristobol's shore. Sea lions lounge
on park benches while we wait for our zodiacs
to churn through the waves. Bring us to our ship,
our Endeavor.

The Voyage Out: The Backstory

Six months before my sixtieth year
I'm diagnosed with breast cancer.
The biopsy reveals it's triple negative.
Meaning nothing positive.

Aggressive, wildly mutating,
strangely behaving cells, not even nourished
by the hormones other breast cancers lap up.
A cancer hard to treat,
harder to survive.

Once shielded and swaddled in bras,
my breast is now radiated redder
than my baby-oil burned body
when I was sixteen, and suffering
for beauty was noble and wise.
I'm carboplatin-infused to a fevered shaking.
My circumference shrinks to twenty city blocks
for six weeks. Then I rejoin the living.
My horizons stretch two hundred miles of familiar
landscape.   But I'm unfamiliar.

Parched islands taunted sailors
who dreamed of water, died of thirst.
In the Galapagos sea iguanas sneeze out
the ocean's salt, swallow its water.
Sea lions claim the beach, indifferent
to human footprints around them.
Tortoises born old carry their shells,
their half-ton bodies, for over a century.

I need the arid equator, the finches selected
to continue their species. The specks 600 miles
west of South American land that flourish
without us.

With Sea Lions

The islands belong to them.
They wear the sand like a shirt.
Its granules scrub their skin clean.
We find one nuzzling and nursing her pup;
a newborn stunned by its birth,
poking mom's belly for a teat.
Her body impresses her exhaustion
into the sand as he latches on.

Our first day out a sea lion spread
across our trail. We spoke softly,
tried to entice him by waving, whistling,
calling, pleading. He stayed.
A line of hikers waited.

They've taken our benches in the square.
We scrounge for rest or warmth.
They stand in our markets, heads tilted up,
eyes expectant as a hound's looking
for carelessness, not love.

In the water we are true strangers. We bob
in waves that warm us, but need our tubes
and masks to watch the ocean's life,
our plastic fins to kick through water.
Their bulky bodies gyrate, ignore currents.
Fishing is their work, their play. Every day.

The Sea Lion Speaks

Like the sloppy lab they left back
home, visitors love me. I'm cute.

My blubber body like a huge baby
they watch somersault. Squeal.

My wide-open eyes, soulful.
My hunts for fish, playful.

They snap their phones. Hundreds
of people hundreds of times.

Their arrow boats paddle into waves.
I swim with them, surface to smiles.

They bask in sunbathing with me.
A friendly creature. Harmless.

Unless his steps get too close,
unless his hands reach to touch my mate

or take the rocky space that is mine.
Then he'll feel my roar chomp

into his thigh, scream while blood
drips into the sand.   He'll understand
what it means to be cute.

Sea Iguanas

Shrunken dinosaurs in Halloween colors
with witches' claws digging into cliffs.
Uglier than ugliness.

But in Chicago a grateful man carried
his 20-pound iguana from a fire.
Kissed its head like a benediction.

You can learn to love anything.
But not everything can love, I tell
myself as the sun begins to set

and the iguanas begin to huddle
on the mountain, curl up
kitten-like, sharing their warmth.

Just a patchwork of camouflage.
Protection, not affection. I know.
But when you want to see caring,

when you want to believe original sin
did not blight this virgin land,
you smile at the heap of reptiles.

You follow the footprints of other travelers
on route to that motorized raft of a boat,
climb in shoulder to shoulder, toe to toe.

Feel your bodies' salt heat, your breaths
almost synchronizing. Eyes being rocked closed.

Threats

The Land Iguana

She isn't going far. Just a quick
run across the sand, her land
where she had grown and she
has found the shallow holes
of turtles' nests, the eggs that feed
her young.

The landscape as bare as the sun is hot.
Shelter, like options, a mirage.
By the time she sees the hawk's
open wings gliding down,
by the time her legs quicken back:
the hawk descends. Its talons clutch.
Knead her cold-blooded body
into heated sand. Pound it into a meal.

The Woman

The store, ten short blocks from my home.
Handbag on my shoulder, the afternoon sun
and a packed sidewalk at my side.
A woman —eyes dark, urgent—stops
me. Speaks a language I'm trying
to learn: *¡Dame! ¡Dame!*

As I try to mentally slow the track
of her syllables, something I recognize
quickens my heart. *¡Dame!*

"*No entiendo*," I say, try to pull away.
Her ample body blocks mine.
Her hand grips my shoulder, and
a screwdriver scrapes my t-shirt,
finds the outline of my ribs.

"Give me your wallet!"

With her command my hand scurries
into my purse, pulls out the money
I give like an offering.

The Post Office Barrel: Innocence

With so little chance of rain wet-rotting
the wood, the only question was how long
a letter would stay in that barrel waiting

for a traveler from London or Canterbury
or Boston to claim it. For a traveler to go
to an unknown address, deliver
this whaler's letter without ever
knowing what its words said.

The bronchitis, I think, will never
leave me again.

Tell Tommy and Johnny to be good boys.
I will do something for them yet.

I expect you are disappointed that
*I am going another season.**

Messages relied on the kindness
of strangers, or on strangers feeling
their lives in the folded papers of others.
A woman waited weeks, months, maybe years
for words that brought sobs of relief
or loss or anger. Whatever the message,
she tucked the letter in a drawer
keeping a piece of him close and safe.

We twenty-first century tourists
risk no high seas, and no one waits to affirm
our lives with our handwriting.

Still, we reenact the ritual. A caller pulls
postcards from the barrel, fills the island's
silence with a litany of places.

Anyone going to Moscow? Santa Monica?
Calgary? Baltimore? We raise our hands
and voices. Take messages.

Mine reads:

Mom,
Having a great time. Hope you get this soon.
                                    Clara

On a day when the smell and light of spring
fill the air, I drive to the leafy detached-home
streets of north Baltimore. True to custom,
I bypass the flagged mailbox, ring the bell,
and wait for her suspicion and puzzlement.

As I explain "Galapagos" "barrel" "postcard,"
she opens the glass door just wide enough
for her hand to reach the card. Smiling,
she turns away and locks her home.

———————

*The excerpts are adapted from letters in *Whaling*
Letters: A Project of the Descendants of Whaling
Masters, Inc., New Bedford, 1980 and 2003.

The Post Office Barrel: Experience

She can't fathom the size of a whale
though she knows the price of light and heat.
She can't fathom the strength of a whale
or the hubris of a slim harpoon against it.

Tides inch out, later encroach on the shore.
Waves peak; thunder breaks the night.
She waits, pulling her shawl over thinning hair.

The children toddle unsteadily; she imagines
the ship rocking. Cracked picture in hand,
she says "Daddy." They learn the word, not the face.

She learns to spin stories of the messenger.
The man like a harpoon flung from the Galapagos
bringing her husband's words and her fate.

She envisions a man traveling from Floreana,
his weathered hand holding a weathered letter.
Her husband writes that he is healthy. The catch

is healthy. Just a few more months till homecoming.
She envisions a man from Floreana, the letter
thin and sallow as his face. Words scrawled in fever.

Halting script that's utterly clear. Death cannot
be proud. Its spoils are tossed to the sea. She
cannot survive the news, but she will.

Remembering Jonah, she wishes a whale
would swallow her husband, spit him on home shores.
She prays for God's grace and God's will.
Forces as mysterious as the ocean's depths.

Lonesome George, Surviving Tortoise

The island I knew was thick green. Bushes,
cacti all there for a stretch of our necks.

The few men that came from the water
kept their distance and their names.

We ate. We slept. Till the changes.
Goats' hooves trampling

through our nests, their mouths wide,
their teeth devouring our brush.

Nothing to do but trudge
up the mountain. Hang on.

One put down her head, never
picked it up. Her shell now a coffin.

Then another. Some died because
there was so little to eat. Some died

because we all die. Finally
I alone was left.

Men found me. Took me to a place
where the food they give is as plentiful

as the brush I remember. They bring me
companions. Young ones. Nimble and easy.

No pasts weighing them down. My species?
They may as well be finches. But one man

sweeps my space. Paces my meals.
Bobs his sagging neck toward mine.

As the tourists watch me, I watch
the wrinkles set into his knobby hands.

Lonesome George Thinking
about the Whalers

Did we think it would stop with one animal?
Even an animal larger than the ships, larger
than our nightmares, is not enough.

Did we think they'd have a pantry of Spam?
Keys primed to open them? That those boards
of salt soaked-cods would multiply
like loaves and fishes?

Yes, they were hungry. But maybe, more,
they were bored with the same swills of food
that never satisfied.

Some tortoises were twice their weight,
the domes of their shells creviced, like the faces
that huddled into their shells. As if there was
something they could tell.

The whalers saw mouthfuls. Pliant cooked meat
steaming fresh. Visions that sent them to desert shores,
sent them pounding over lava for all of us.

Men stacked tortoises like bulky rations,
filled every crevice. So far from any land
they knew, so far from any land, they never
even tried to escape. Their wondrous meat

was sweet and succulent as dry land.
Those tortoises died for Whalemen,
who bring light to the world.

Looking at a Blue-Footed Booby

after Wallace Stevens

1

A clown's foot,
webbed
and bright,
ready
to be tripped over.

2

A child pressing
down on the crayon that
bleeds blue
in the white space.

3

The color of pixie candy, or
granules like fairy dust
sprinkled on a fading Tinkerbell
fluttering her wings.

4

A baby booty knitted
right into the skin.

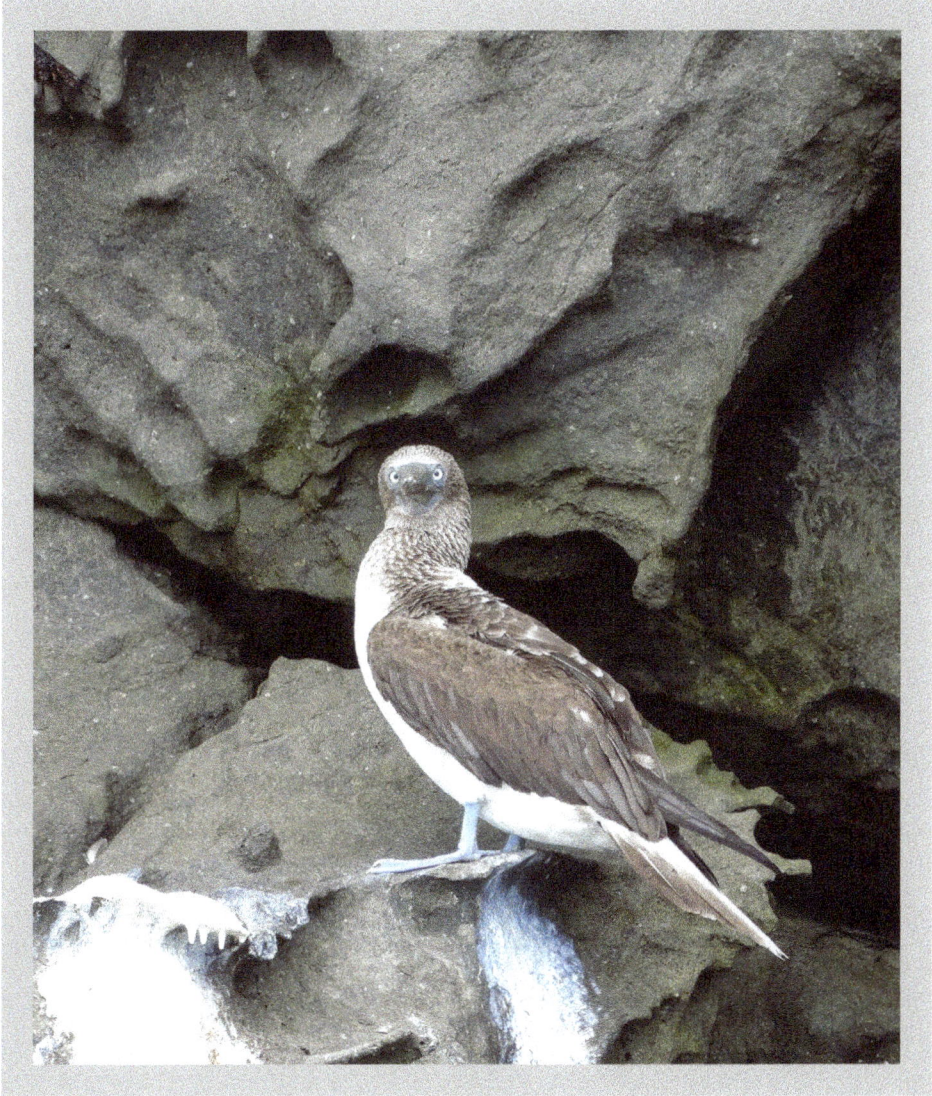

5

Test the blue feet first,
especially if you fly.
Wait before you let
strange colors tint your body.

6

Why aren't all feet blue?
Why do
blue-breasted jays
perch over paper-
bag brown feet?

7

We ponder your feet.
Forgetting you can fly.

8

Things as they are
are changed with the tint of blue.
And you thought it was the music.

9

A baby's open eyes;
its dewy skin glazed with tears.
We all cuddle hope.

10

The blues. The ache
of another man done wrong.
Understood. But what
did the color blue
do to you?

11

As my skin thins to filo
my veins assert themselves.
Faint aqua lines stretching out.

12

In Chicago a Tiffany dome
flanked by great white men
filters the sky
through geometric designs.

13

The Pacific Ocean isn't big
enough for blue.
Color permeates the sky.
Dapples its creatures.

Blue-Footed Boobys:
After *A Christmas Carol*

Boobys past: Males court with twigs.
Circle their chosen mates in those dances
that pull tourists' faces into smiles.
Nests of boobys follow, and these birds,
monogamous as church ladies,
nudge flock after flock into flight.

Boobys present: They carry on, or try.
Fly, swoop for schools of sardines
precious as potatoes in Ireland,
but appearing less frequently
every year. Schools thin like
classrooms facing COVID.
One booby starved to death,
his stiff feathers masked
a protruding rib cage.

Boobys future: Nests never built.
The beach swallows the last
blue-webbed feet still tingling
with the memory of dance. We have
other birds. Hearty pliable holdouts.
The same few we count on one hand
everywhere. The earth's shopping mall
of species. Until, slowly, one after another
stiffens into the sand.

Seeing Albatrosses on Espanola, Thinking of Wisdom on Midway Atoll

Who would want eternal life?
Body and brain empty as gourds.
Purpose as cloudy as our eyes.
We want the body running steady
in the stride it found around age 25.
We want it nesting, foraging with
a purpose it doesn't need to name.
But wakes to every morning
as our limbs stretch out and we launch.

Wisdom is our patron saint.
Without in vitro or a surrogate,
without a novena or a pilgrimage
she's defied nature's own
toughest odds. Again.
Hatched her 40th chick at age 66.

No poison plastic or lead,
no tsunami or food shortages.
Not even the humdrum slow-
down of age itself could stop her.

She's never tired of settling
an egg under her warm butt,
of finding squid for a ready open beak,
or of that same sleek-backed partner
sharing chores like a Nordic dad.
Launching one more albatross,
one more, one more, until death.

Reconsidering Coleridge's Albatross

Yanked out of time with that rime,
memorialized as a millstone weighing
down a killer's neck. We see in
its rigid body, its vacant charcoal eyes
marks of a sailor's penance,
products of his madness. As though
that bird chose to be murdered so
it could torment a man and we could
just disregard the bird's 60-year lifespan
that sailor's arrow shredded through.
No one knows the bird's sprint to flight.
The wingspan that's an elephant's height.
These blue waters wash us in ourselves.
We know our own stories. Nothing else.

Walter J. Enright. Pix. N.

Birders Looking for Finches

for Christine

So ordinary they startle.
Remind me of sparrows
fluttering near feeders.

So unlike flamingos,
with shrimp-pink feathers
and tall-twig legs.

Or penguins, oddly equatorial.
Enticing swimmers with play,
or sunning on rock crags.

Far from cities, searching
for nature's rarities, I've no
patience for homespun finches.

But the birders wake early.
Watch, wait as light spreads.
Listen. They have learned

to distinguish cries from calls.
Name criers and callers
while others hear just noise.

They know that epiphanies
spring from the mundane.
That the length of a species'

beak reveals the key
to its survival. To what they
are and what they've lost.

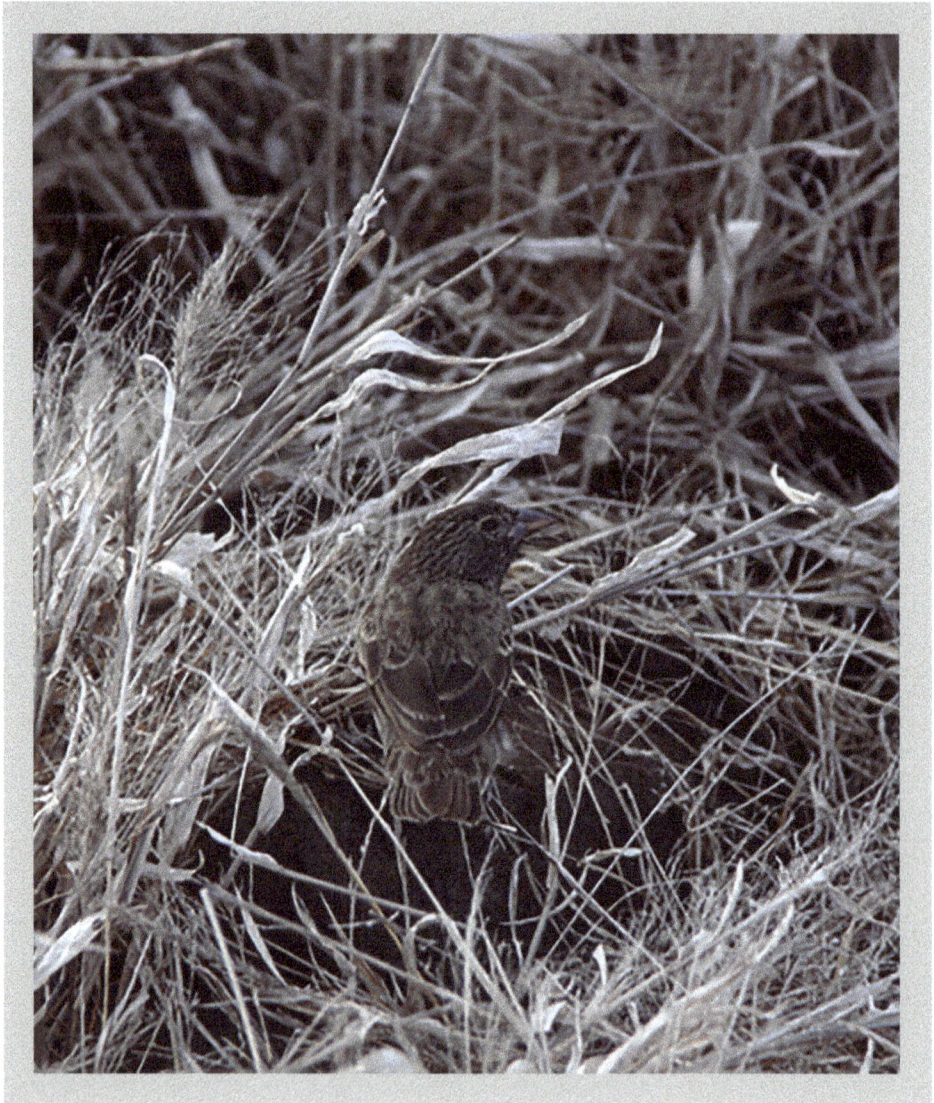

Death of the Finches

They weathered rains
that flooded the islands.
Their beaks honed themselves
to short-trimmed instruments.
Until drought cracked through soil.
Then their beaks thickened, sharpened.
True, many carcasses were churned
into the soil. But enough lived.
Enough bred. Many more thrived.

Now, it's not a natural cataclysm.
Not an owl silently swooping down
or a cat pouncing at the nest.

It's a fly, and not even an adult
fully-flying fly that's killing finches.
It's the larvae left inside nests.
Deforming those survivor beaks.
Sucking blood from chicks
who cannot defend or adapt
but only weaken and die.

What do the mothers know?
As they watch their babes
shrivel in their grass home?
Do they see human folly
ignoring the cocooned parasite
that sucks the downy chicks dry?

Open Waters

At birth, our gills
are long gone.
The rhythm of rocking

in water forgotten. Especially
if, like me, you're in
a land-bound family.

Spending days at the beach
braving knee-scraping waves.
Wading out of pools

in our line-dry bathing suits.
I watched other children
cannonball, swim below

the water's surface. Slowly,
I found the courage
to find water ways.

To alternate my arms, pace
my breaths. Kick legs shaking
and sinking for a pool's length.

Later to stretch out my arms, rotate
my head in open waters. Let
the ocean's sun and salt

exfoliate my skin. And
most difficult,
most astonishing:

To float.
Lie back.
Let go.

Diving

O you who turn the wheel and look to windward,
Consider Phlebas, who was once handsome and tall as you.
—"Death by Water," The Waste Land

1

Twenty-three years old, slight but strong, master diver,
avid diver. Mind throbbing with deep-sea images,
she pairs off with a partner, takes a deep breath, dives.

2

Schools of hammerheads appear without warning.
All angles and points, a wall of writhing barbwire.
Sinister. Hypnotic. Swaying, riding the sea.

3

Fourteen divers transfixed, chasing the same sea lion.
Skill and adrenaline guide them through opaque waters.
But a curtain of their air bubbles blocks vision.

4

The waters, so cold, teem with currents and rip tides.
She has 150 dives: notches in a novice belt.
Some advice: Hang onto rocks. Hang onto your life.

5

These currents nurture life. Swirling round the archipelago,
carrying larvae, plankton, even small animals,
sustaining diversity, sustaining wonder.

6

She took a deep breath, jumped backward into the sea,
swam with a partner, fought the undertow, until she was lost.
The expedition stopped while divers waited, then searched.

7

They found her with her mask off, her regulator
out of her mouth. Curled in a fetal position,
her face peaceful. Accepting the deep sea swell.

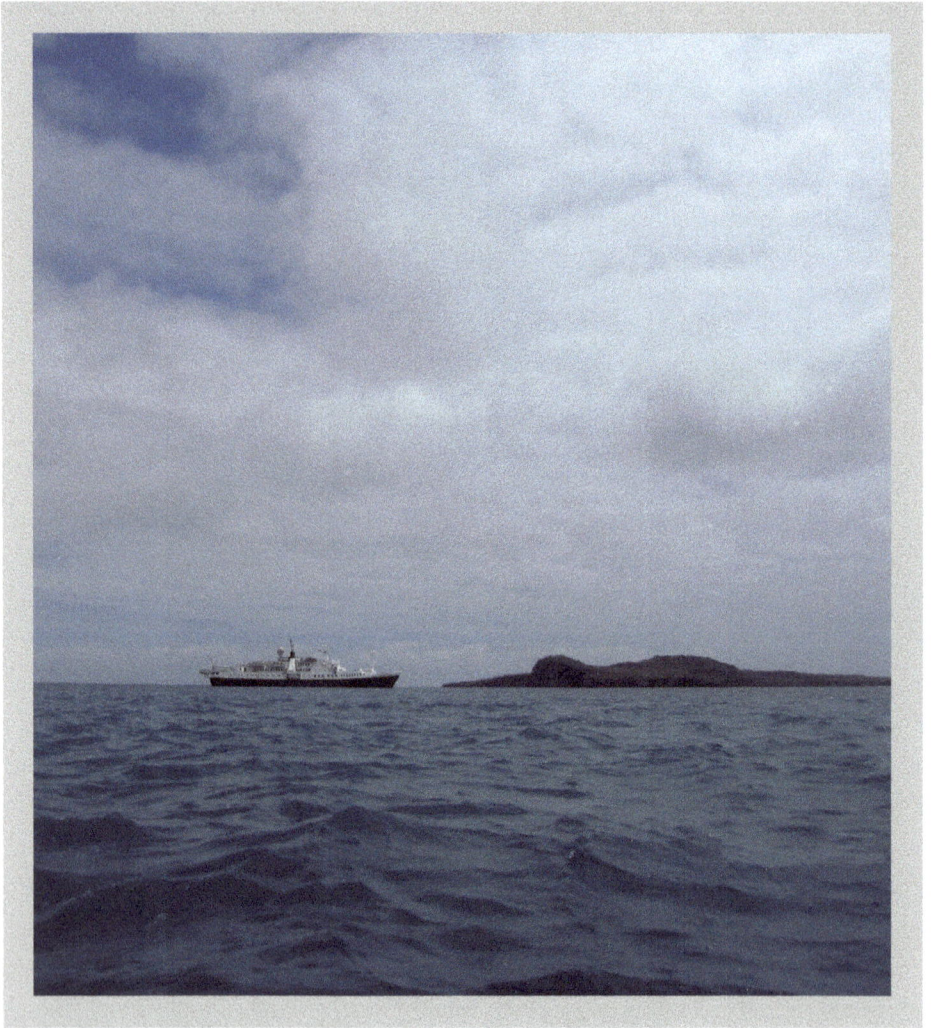

The Voyage Home: Questions

What happens to a dream achieved?

Is it a check on the list
                    prompting you for more?

An answered prayer
                    moving you to tears?

Does it make you sit back, sigh,
                    walk away head held high?

Or is it a portal
                    to another dream?

To a nightmare
                    the shadow side

lurking behind
                    the photo album?

I smile at all I've seen
                    but cringe at all I learned.

Don't want to but I ponder
                    what now that I've returned?

After such knowledge,
                    what words?
                    what acts?

After such knowledge,
                    what forgiveness?

Writing about the Galapagos

after W. B. Yeats

The albatrosses of legends lingered
on Española, postponing December migration.

The clownish seals that protect fiercely
as Rottweilers shared their water and our benches.

Sea iguanas, land iguanas, cold-blooded
survivors, ignored us like we were rocks.

Lumbering tortoises drew us to Santa Cruz,
to the cooler mountains and muddy grassy steps.

The Pacific itself, precarious cradle of life—
Galapagos, you have not deserted me.

Your images are impressed on my urban mind.
They shape my poems, shape my knowledge.

If I struggle to separate the painted stages
and the players from the lives themselves, it is

because their pulses, the rhythms of their terrain
and water resist a snapshot poem.

Resist, perhaps, my human offerings to nature
that never references itself. And I

have not deserted these isles, even if words
stick in my pen, if the lines on the screen

affirm my frustration. My writing relearns
its own cycle: leave and return.

About the Author

MICHELLE M. TOKARCZYK has authored two poetry books: *The House I'm Running From* and *Bronx Migrations*. Her work has also been published in numerous journals and anthologies such as the *minnesota review, The Skinny Poetry Journal, Unearthed, Masque & Spectacle, Oyster River Pages, Evening Street Review, and Where We Stand: Poems of Black Resilience* (Cherry Castle Publishing). Her poems have been nominated for Pushcart and Best of the Net Prizes. Tokarczyk is a professor emerita of English at Goucher College (Baltimore, Maryland).
—mmtokarczyk.wixsite.com/mysite

www.ingramcontent.com/pod-product-compliance
Lightning Source LLC
Chambersburg PA
CBHW050824090426
42738CB00021B/3478